W9-BHS-858

The Hoover Dam

by Meish Goldish

Consultant:
Shirl R. Naegle MS, Collections Manager
Boulder City/Hoover Dam Museum
Boulder City, Nevada

BEARPORT
PUBLISHING

New York, New York

Credits

Cover, © Andrew Zarivny/Shutterstock; 2–3, © Stefano Politi Markovina/Alamy; 4, US NARA/tinyurl.com/zpvloeo/Public domain; 5, © Mapping Specialists, Ltd.; 6T, Internet Archive Book Images/tinyurl.com/j845t9j/Public domin; 6B, © ArnaudS2/Shutterstock; 7T, © Ulrich Mueller/Shutterstock; 7B, Margaret Luzier, USACE/tinyurl.com/jname8t/Public Domain; 8, © Joseph Sohm/Shutterstock; 9L, © John Elk III/Alamy; 9R, Library of Congress; 10, © Everett Historical/Shutterstock; 11T, UNLV Libraries, Special Collections; 11B, © Sueddeutsche Zeitung Photo/Alamy; 12, © Mapping Specialists, Ltd.; 13, US NARA/tinyurl.com/hodlvjw/Public domain; 14, US NARA/tinyurl.com/pfwfvmh/Public domain; 15, US NARA/tinyurl.com/hv2t4rf/Public domain; 16, © Peter Gudella/Shutterstock; 17T, US NARA/tinyurl.com/hcryxbp/Public domain; 17B, US NARA/tinyurl.com/ha78r2m/Public domain; 18, US NARA/tinyurl.com/ha78r2m/Shutterstock; 19, USBR/tinyurl.com/zp3oqzb/Public domain; 20, © jiawangkun/Shutterstock; 21, © Scott Prokop/Shutterstock; 22, Tomia/tinyurl.com/halrceo/CC BY-SA 3.0; 23T, © Jerry Callaghan/Shutterstock; 23B, © Sarah Fields Photography/Shutterstock; 24L, © GL Archive/Alamy; 24R, Library of Congress; 25, David Herrera/tinyurl.com/hapzul4/CC BY 2.0; 26TL, © Steve Byland/Shutterstock; 26BL, © Don Mammoser/Alamy; 26R, Lake Mead NRA Public Affairs/tinyurl.com/zmzqk3z/CC BY-SA 2.0; 27, © Andrew Zarivny/Shutterstock; 28–29, © Andrew Zarivny/Shutterstock; 31, © Eddie_/Shutterstock; 32, © Bryan Busovicki/Shutterstock.

Publisher: Kenn Goin
Editor: Jessica Rudolph
Creative Director: Spencer Brinker
Photo Researcher: Editorial Directions, Inc.

Library of Congress Cataloging-in-Publication Data

Names: Goldish, Meish, author.
Title: The Hoover Dam / by Meish Goldish.
Description: New York, New York : Bearport Publishing, [2017] | Series: American places: from vision to reality | Includes bibliographical references and index.
Identifiers: LCCN 2016020320 | ISBN 9781944102456 (library binding)Subjects: LCSH: Hoover Dam (Ariz. and Nev.)—Juvenile literature. | Dams—Design and construction—Juvenile literature. | Water-supply—Southwest, New—Juvenile literature.
Classification: LCC TC557.5.H6 G65 2017 | DDC 627/.820979313—dc23
LC record available at https://lccn.loc.gov/2016020320

Copyright © 2017 Bearport Publishing Company, Inc. All rights reserved. No part of this publication may be reproduced in whole or in part, stored in any retrieval system, or transmitted in any form or by any means, electronic, mechanical, photocopying, recording, or otherwise, without written permission from the publisher.

For more information, write to Bearport Publishing Company, Inc., 45 West 21st Street, Suite 3B, New York, New York 10010.
Printed in the United States of America.

10 9 8 7 6 5 4 3 2 1

Contents

Canyon of Danger

On a spring day in 1933, a group of workers hung from long ropes along the walls of the Black **Canyon**, dangerously high above the Colorado River. The men were in a desert on the border between Arizona and Nevada—one of the hottest and driest areas of the United States. Using **jackhammers**, the workers, called high scalers, drilled holes into the rock. One wrong move could mean disaster.

High scalers drilled holes about 3 inches (7.6 cm) wide and at least 3 feet (1 m) deep.

A high scaler with a jackhammer

After the drilling was done, other workers called powder monkeys carefully placed **dynamite** into the holes. Then everyone took shelter, and the blasts were set off. Boom! Boom! The earsplitting noise echoed off the canyon walls. When the cloud of dirt and dust cleared, the men returned to remove any loose rock that stuck to the **cliffs**. What were these brave workers doing? They were building one of the biggest structures in the world—the Hoover **Dam**.

Workers at Black Canyon risked their lives to build the Hoover Dam. Handling dynamite was dangerous, and falling rocks could injure or kill a person.

A Wild River

Why was there a need for such a huge dam? It was difficult for people to live or work near the lower Colorado River. In spring, melted snow and heavy rain sometimes caused the river to flood. Its **raging** waters often destroyed homes and crops. Then, in summer, very little rain fell. The land dried up, and many crops died from lack of water.

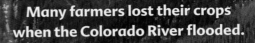

Many farmers lost their crops when the Colorado River flooded.

Melted snow from the Rocky Mountains runs into streams and small rivers that eventually flow into the Colorado River.

A large, strong dam could solve many problems. It would hold back the river's rising water and prevent floods. It would also create a new lake for farmers to use to water their crops, and for people to use for drinking and washing. The dam could also be used to make electricity for people living in the Southwest.

Before the 1930s, people had built dams made of earth and mud along the Colorado River. However, over time, the river's powerful waters destroyed the dams.

Dams can help provide water for growing crops.

There are thousands of dams in the United States. This dam is in West Virginia.

Choosing the Right Place

Starting in 1920, **surveyors** for the U.S. government began to search for the best place to build the dam. The dam needed to be tall in order to hold back a huge amount of water. So, government workers visited deep, narrow canyons along the Colorado River. They measured the height and width of the cliffs.

Surveyors use special equipment to study rivers and the lands they run through.

Government workers also rode on rafts and drilled into the river bottom to test the hardness of the **bedrock**. If a canyon's walls and bedrock had many faults, or cracks, they would be too weak to hold the weight of the dam. Eventually, Black Canyon was chosen as the site for the Hoover Dam. Its cliffs and bedrock have few faults and are very strong.

This photo from the late 1800s shows the Black Canyon.

The Colorado River has very strong rapids, and riding a raft on it can be risky.

In 1922, a surveyor named J.G. Tierney died when he fell off his raft and drowned. Unfortunately, this was only the first of many deaths that occurred during the dangerous project.

Living in Ragtown

The next step in building the dam was hiring workers—about 5,000 of them! Finding enough men was no problem, since Americans were living through the Great Depression. Many people were out of work and desperate to find jobs. However, housing the workers and their families in the desert would be a big problem. There were no towns with houses or hotels nearby. Workers were forced to create settlements and build homes out of whatever materials they could find.

The Great Depression was a time of **economic** hardship that lasted throughout the 1930s. During that time, one out of every four American workers was out of a job.

Some people who were out of work sold fruit on the street.

Some workers used blankets, cardboard, or wood to make tents or shacks. The collection of homes in one of the settlements was known as Ragtown. Life in Ragtown wasn't easy. There was no electricity or **sanitation**. People had to walk to the river to get water, and the desert heat was fierce. One worker said, "It was rough. It got so hot that when you'd pick up the knives and forks, you'd want to put your gloves on."

A worker's family living in a shack in Ragtown in 1931

In 1932, workers and their families moved to Boulder City, Nevada, a town built by the U.S. government. The town had better homes and cleaner water.

A Rocky Start

Work on the Hoover Dam began in the spring of 1931. The first job was to stop the Colorado River from flowing through the canyon area where the dam would be built. To do that, workers needed to carve out four huge tunnels in the canyon's walls. The tunnels would steer the river away from its normal path so workers could then build the dam on dry land.

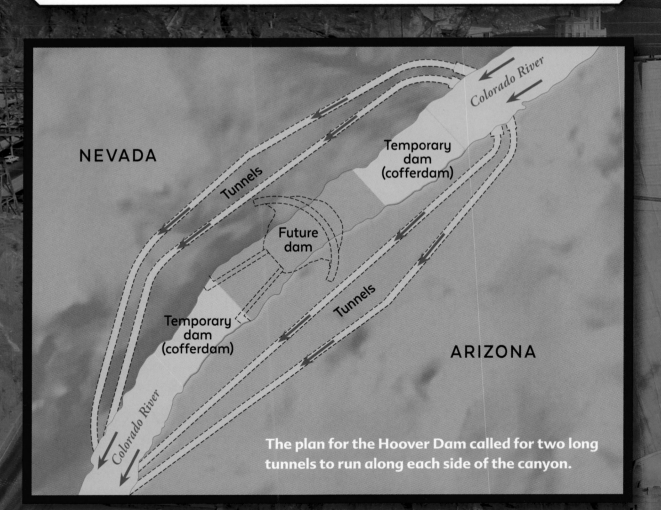

NEVADA

Colorado River

Tunnels

Temporary dam (cofferdam)

Future dam

Temporary dam (cofferdam)

Tunnels

ARIZONA

Colorado River

The plan for the Hoover Dam called for two long tunnels to run along each side of the canyon.

To create each tunnel, drillers rode on the back of vehicles called jumbo trucks, which had three levels of platforms. The men stood on the platforms and drilled holes—up to 30 at a time—into the canyon's walls. Then they filled the holes with dynamite and blasted the rock away.

Work at the site went on night and day. Men worked 40 hours a week in different **shifts**. The only days off were Christmas and the Fourth of July.

The jumbo trucks had three levels so that many men could drill into different parts of the cliff at the same time, making the job go faster.

Moving the River

Over time, the four tunnels grew enormous. Each one was about 4,000 feet (1,219 m) long and 56 feet (17 m) high—that's as tall as a five-story building! The inner walls and ceilings were lined with 3 feet (1 m) of **concrete** to keep them from caving in. After 14 months, all four tunnels were completed.

Several men who worked in the tunnels died from **heat exhaustion**. The temperature inside a tunnel could climb to 130°F (54°C).

Each tunnel was about as long as 11 football fields placed end to end!

Next, workers used bulldozers and dump trucks to pile a huge mound of rocks and dirt into the riverbed. This temporary dam, called a **cofferdam**, jammed the river, forcing its water to flow into the tunnels. A second cofferdam on the other side of the dam site kept the river from washing back into the work area. With all the water out of the way, the dam could now be built on dry land.

Shaping the Canyon

Workers then had to shape and smooth the cliff walls. This would allow the concrete dam to fit perfectly against the canyon's rock walls. **Engineers** had designed the Hoover Dam to be an **arch dam**. Its U-shaped curve, set tightly between the canyon walls, would give the dam extra strength to hold back the powerful Colorado River.

This arch dam is in Australia.

As water pushes against the curved wall of an arch dam, the ends of the dam push into the canyon walls, creating a tight fit.

To shape the cliffs, high scalers drilled holes in the canyon walls, and then powder monkeys blasted the holes with dynamite. The drilling and blasting went on for months. Later, workers used **steam shovels** to dig deep into the dry riverbed. At 135 feet (41 m) down, they hit bedrock—the solid **foundation** that would hold the dam's tremendous weight.

High scalers hanging on ropes

High scalers working hundreds of feet above the riverbed

Large trucks carried away tons of loose rock and dirt from the work site.

Building Blocks

With the canyon walls and foundation ready, workers began to construct the dam in June 1933. Concrete for the dam was made at factories, then trains carried it to the nearby building site. Giant buckets of wet concrete were lifted by a cable over the foundation, then the concrete was placed into a square-shaped wooden form. When the material dried, the form was removed, leaving a hard block that was 5 feet (1.5 m) high. Each day hundreds of buckets of concrete were poured.

Workers placing the concrete into forms

Workers attached the blocks to one another with **grout**. The **interlocking** blocks fit together like the bricks of a house. Block by block, the dam grew taller and wider. When the last of the concrete was poured in May 1935, the dam stood 726 feet (221 m) high. It was 1,244 feet (379 m) wide at the top, and weighed 6.6 million tons (6 million metric tons).

The Hoover Dam was made with enough concrete to build a 4-foot-wide (1.2 m) sidewalk

A New Lake

Once the concrete dam was finished, workers plugged three of the tunnels that carried the river water around the dam with concrete. The fourth tunnel was blocked with a heavy gate, and the lower cofferdam was removed. With the tunnels closed, the Colorado River began to flow along its regular path. The upper cofferdam, which was left in place, was soon covered with water. Because the river was held back by the large dam, a huge lake—called Lake Mead—formed behind the wall.

Boats docked near the shore

Lake Mead, which stretches 120 miles (193 km) behind the dam, is the largest man-made lake in the United States. Visitors can go swimming, fishing, and sailing at the lake.

Lake Mead serves many purposes. Some of its water is sent along **canals** and pipes to Arizona, Nevada, and California. The water **irrigates** farmland that would otherwise be too dry for farming. Some water flows through pipes to cities and towns in the Southwest. More than 20 million people use the lake's water for drinking, cooking, and washing.

Intake towers

When water from Lake Mead is ready to be sent to cities and farms, workers at the dam open intake towers. Water flows into the towers and then into pipes and canals that transport the water.

Making Electricity

In addition to the dam, workers built two **power plants**, one on the Arizona side of the Colorado River and one on the Nevada side. The two plants use water from Lake Mead to make electricity. Water first flows through the intake towers and into the power plants. Then the water rushes into giant machines, creating electricity.

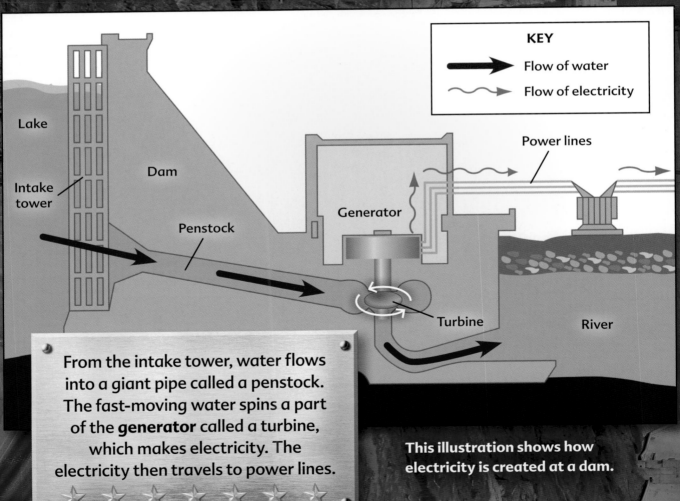

KEY

Flow of water

Flow of electricity

Lake

Dam

Intake tower

Penstock

Generator

Power lines

Turbine

River

From the intake tower, water flows into a giant pipe called a penstock. The fast-moving water spins a part of the **generator** called a turbine, which makes electricity. The electricity then travels to power lines.

This illustration shows how electricity is created at a dam.

Electricity travels through power lines to office buildings, homes, factories, and other places in the Southwest. The two power plants at the Hoover Dam make enough electricity for 1.3 million people!

Electricity made at the Hoover Dam travels though wires (right), and lights up desert cities such as Los Angeles, California (below).

Opening Day

When the Hoover Dam officially opened on September 30, 1935, it was the largest dam in the world. To mark its opening, President Franklin D. Roosevelt made a speech in front of 20,000 people. He called the dam "an engineering victory . . . another great achievement of American **resourcefulness**, skill, and determination."

Franklin D. Roosevelt served as president from 1933 to 1945.

The Hoover Dam was once called Boulder Dam. In 1947, it was officially renamed to honor Herbert Hoover, who served as president from 1929 to 1933.

Many people in the crowd were dam workers. They knew better than anyone else the struggles that went into finishing the project. During the five years it took to build the dam, more than 100 workers lost their lives. They died from falling rocks, heat exhaustion, drowning, explosions, and accidents involving heavy equipment.

THEY·DIED·TO·MAKE THE·DESERT·BLOOM

Visitors to the Hoover Dam can view art that honors the men who died while working on the project.

The Hoover Dam Today

Today, the Hoover Dam continues to do exactly what it was built to do. Since the dam opened, the lower Colorado River has never flooded. Water from Lake Mead creates electricity and irrigates farmland as far away as Mexico. The dam has helped Southwestern cities to grow. Without water and electricity, it would be impossible for large cities to thrive in the desert.

Many kinds of wildlife come to Lake Mead for water. The lake attracts bighorn sheep, coyotes, and bobcats, as well as tortoises, lizards, and snakes.

Rattlesnake

Bobcat

Bighorn sheep

Visitors from all over the world visit the Hoover Dam. They can even take a tour to learn about its history and how the power plants work. Although it is no longer the world's biggest dam, the Hoover Dam remains a remarkable structure that has improved the lives of millions of people.

Lake Mead

Bridge

Dam

The Mike O'Callaghan-Pat Tillman Memorial Bridge opened at the Hoover Dam in 2010. The bridge helps move the flow of traffic between Arizona and Nevada.

The Hoover Dam
BY THE NUMBERS

Width at Top: 1,244 feet (379 m)

Height: 726 feet (221 m)

About 8.5 million pounds (3.9 million kg) of dynamite were used to blast the tunnels and dam foundation.

The greatest number of workers on the job at one time was 5,218.

Thickness at Top: 45 feet (14 m)

Weight: 6.6 million tons (6 million metric tons)

Thickness at Bottom: 660 feet (201 m)

Cost to Build: $54.7 million

Glossary

arch dam (ARCH DAM) a solid dam made of concrete that is curved in the middle

bedrock (BED-rok) the solid layer of rock under the soil and loose rock

canals (kuh-NALZ) human-made waterways

canyon (KAN-yuhn) a deep, narrow valley carved out by a river

cliffs (KLIFSS) high, steep rocks

cofferdam (KAW-fur-dam) a temporary dam that is built to allow workers to build another, larger dam on dry ground

concrete (kon-KREET) a mixture of sand, water, cement, and gravel that is used in construction

dam (DAM) a solid wall built across a river to hold back water

dynamite (DYE-nuh-mite) a powerful explosive that is used to blow things up during construction

economic (eh-kuh-NOM-ihk) having to do with money and how goods are bought and sold

engineers (en-juh-NIHRZ) people who design and construct buildings, machines, bridges, and roads

foundation (foun-DAY-shuhn) a solid structure on which a building is constructed

generator (JEN-uh-ray-tur) a machine that produces electricity

grout (GROUT) a thin type of concrete; a mixture of cement, water, and fine sand, which binds building blocks together

heat exhaustion (HEET eg-ZAWS-chuhn) a condition caused by extreme heat that can lead to cramps, stroke, or death

interlocking (IN-tur-*lok*-ing) fitting tightly together

irrigates (IHR-ih-gayts) waters the land so crops can grow on it

jackhammers (JAK-ham-urz) drilling machines that break up rock

power plants (POU-ur PLANTS) factories that produce electricity

raging (RAY-jing) wild or angry

resourcefulness (rih-ZORSS-fuhl-nuhss) the ability to know how to deal with difficulties

sanitation (*san*-uh-TAY-shuhn) practices that promote cleanliness and prevention of diseases, including getting rid of body waste in a manner that doesn't pollute drinking water

shifts (SHIFTS) set periods of time that people work

steam shovels (STEEM SHUHV-uhlz) giant digging machines powered by steam, gas, or electricity

surveyors (sur-VAY-urz) people who measure the position, height, and shape of land

Bibliography

DuTemple, Lesley A. *The Hoover Dam (Great Building Feats).* Minneapolis, MN: Lerner (2003).

Hiltzik, Michael. *Colossus: Hoover Dam and the Making of the American Century.* New York: Free Press (2010).

Lusted, Marcia. *The Hoover Dam (Building History Series).* Farmington Hills, MI: Lucent Books (2003).

Read More

Graham, Ian. *You Wouldn't Want to Work on the Hoover Dam!: An Explosive Job You'd Rather Not Do.* New York: Franklin Watts (2012).

Mann, Elizabeth. *Hoover Dam (Wonders of the World).* New York: Mikaya Press (2001).

Zuehlke, Jeffrey. *The Hoover Dam (Lightning Bolt Books: Famous Places).* Minneapolis, MN: Lerner (2010).

Learn More Online

To learn more about the Hoover Dam, visit:
www.bearportpublishing.com/AmericanPlaces

Index

About the Author

Meish Goldish is an award-winning author of more than 300 books for children. This is his 100th book for Bearport Publishing. He lives in Brooklyn, New York.